KT-556-991

Fife Council Education Department
King's Road Primary School
King's Crescent, Rosyth KY11 2RS

WHAT IS WEATHER?

Rain

Miranda Ashwell and Andy Owen

Heinemann
LIBRARY

First published in Great Britain by Heinemann Library,
Halley Court, Jordan Hill, Oxford OX2 8EJ,
a division of Reed Educational and Professional Publishing Ltd.
Heinemann is a registered trademark of Reed Educational & Professional Publishing Limited.

OXFORD MELBOURNE AUCKLAND
JOHANNESBURG BLANTYRE GABORONE
IBADAN PORTSMOUTH NH (USA) CHICAGO

Designed by David Oakley
Printed and bound in Hong Kong/China.

03 02 01 00
10 9 8 7 6 5 4 3 2

ISBN 0 431 03822 8

British Library Cataloguing in Publication Data

> Ashwell, Miranda
> What is rain?. - (What is weather?)
> 1. Rain and rainfall - Juvenile literature
> I. Title II. Owen, Andy
> 551.5'77
>
> ISBN 0431038228

Acknowledgements
The Publishers would like to thank the following for permission to reproduce photographs:
Bruce Coleman Limited: E Bjurstrom p28, M Boulton p26, J Cancalosi p27, A Compost p18, S Krasemann p11, F Prenzel p29, H Reinhard p25, K Rushby p21; FLPA: C Mattison p19; Robert Harding Picture Library: pp4, 7, J Francillon p30, J Miller p9; Oxford Scientific Films: S Olwe p15, K Wothe p17; Andy Owen: p8; Panos Pictures: J-L Dugasi p22; Planet Earth Pictures: R Salm p16; Tony Stone Images: P Cutler p5; Still Pictures: M Edwards p20, P Gleizes p10, M Gunther p12, R Pfortner p24, A Watson p13; Telegraph Colour Library: C Mellor p14, A Mo p23.

Cover: C Brunskill, Allsport.

Every effort has been made to contact copyright holders of any material reproduced in this book. Any omissions will be rectified in subsequent printings if notice is given to the Publisher.

Any words appearing in the text in bold, **like this**, are explained in the Glossary.

Contents

What is rain?

Rain is water. It falls from clouds. Clouds are made of lots and lots of tiny drops of water. Rain is falling from this cloud into the sea.

Rain makes everything wet. When lots of rain falls in a short time, we say that it is raining heavily.

Why does it rain?

The air is full of tiny drops of water but they are too small to see. Sometimes there are so many drops that the air feels damp. We might even see some **mist**.

When the air cools, the water drops join together. These larger water drops make clouds in the sky which we can see. The water drops fall out of the sky as rain.

Where does it rain?

The wind carries clouds over high ground where the air is cold. The cold air turns the water drops in the clouds into falling rain.

It rains when damp air cools. In
rainforests it rains almost every day.
The warm, damp air rises. As it rises it
cools, making clouds and heavy rain.

Low clouds and frozen rain

Clouds sometimes lie near to the ground. This is called **fog**. Driving in fog is dangerous. It is hard to see where you are going.

This is **hail**. Hail falls when water in clouds gets very cold. It freezes into hard pieces of ice.

Wet or dry

Rainforests have more rain than anywhere else in the world. It rains nearly every day in these hot, wet forests.

It may not rain for years in a **desert**. Deserts can be hot or cold, but they are always very dry places.

13

Rain patterns

Rain comes at the same time every year in some places. After months without rain, the streets of cities in India are very hot and dusty.

When the rain comes it falls very heavily. It lasts for several months. People use the rain-water to help grow their food.

Life in dry places

All animals need water to live. This camel lives where there is very little rain. It can live without water for longer than most animals, but it must drink sometimes.

Plants need water to grow or they will **wilt** and die. These plants are used to living in **deserts**. They store water inside their thick **stems**.

Life in wet places

Plants in the **rainforest** get plenty of rain. The rain and sunshine help the plants to grow very large. They also grow very quickly.

The leaves of rainforest plants get very wet. The rain flows along the shiny leaves. Frogs live in the tiny pools of water held by the leaves.

Drinking water

The water we drink comes from rain-water. We all need to drink water. Our water comes out of taps, but some people have to collect water to take home.

When it rains, rain-water soaks into the ground. A hole has been dug to reach the water here. People use the water themselves and also give it to their animals.

Collecting rain-water

Our rain-water is held in **reservoirs**. When it has not rained for many months, there is not much water left in the reservoirs. People have used most of the water.

After weeks of rain the reservoir is full of water. The water is carried to a city in huge pipes. It is used in homes and **factories**.

Dirty rain

Smoke from **factories** makes the air dirty. Some of the dirt gets into water drops and falls with the rain. We call this **acid rain**.

Acid rain harms many living things. These trees are dying because acid rain has fallen here for many years.

Too much rain

Rivers flow with rain-water. After heavy rain, water can spill out of the river and onto the land. We call this a **flood**.

The flood-water flows into houses and people can be trapped. Fast-flowing flood-water can sweep away anything in its path.

Too little rain

When there is no rain the soil dries out. Most plants cannot live for long without water. They soon **wilt** and die.

A **drought** is when it does not rain for a long time. Animals die when they cannot find drinking water.

It's amazing!

Sometimes we see lightning when it rains. Lightning is a huge spark of electricity which lights up the sky. Thunder rumbles as the air heats up quickly.

Glossary

acid rain   rain that has become mixed with smoke from factories and cars. It can damage plants and buildings.

desert   a place where there is very little rain

drought   a long time without rain

factory   a place where people make things

flood   when the land is covered by water

fog   when the air is so full of drops of water that it is difficult to see very far

hail   rain that falls as drops of ice

rainforest   thick forest which grows in hot, rainy places

reservoir   a place where water is stored

mist   when it is damp and cold, we can sometimes see the drops of water in the air

stem   the part of a plant from which the leaves and flowers grow

wilt   when plants have no water their leaves become limp and they die

Index